Why can't I look like my best friend?

Because no one in the world looks quite like you.

Everyone has a head, body, legs and arms, but there are some things that make everyone look different.

You get the colour of your hair, skin and eyes from your parents. The way you look is a mixture of your mother and father.

Why won't my body bend all over?

Because your bones can't bend.

There are hundreds of strong, hard bones inside your body. Your body would be floppy without them.

You can only bend your body at places where two bones meet. These places are called joints.

Why can't I watch TV all day?

Because your body works best if you use it.

Walking, running and jumping makes your bones and muscles stronger. Moving about helps your heart and lungs work better.

Why can't my heart ever have a rest?

Because if your heart stopped, so would you.

Your heart is like a pump
that never stops beating
and never gets tired.

Every time your heart beats,
it pushes blood around your body.
The blood is full of goodness
from the air you breathe
and the food you eat.

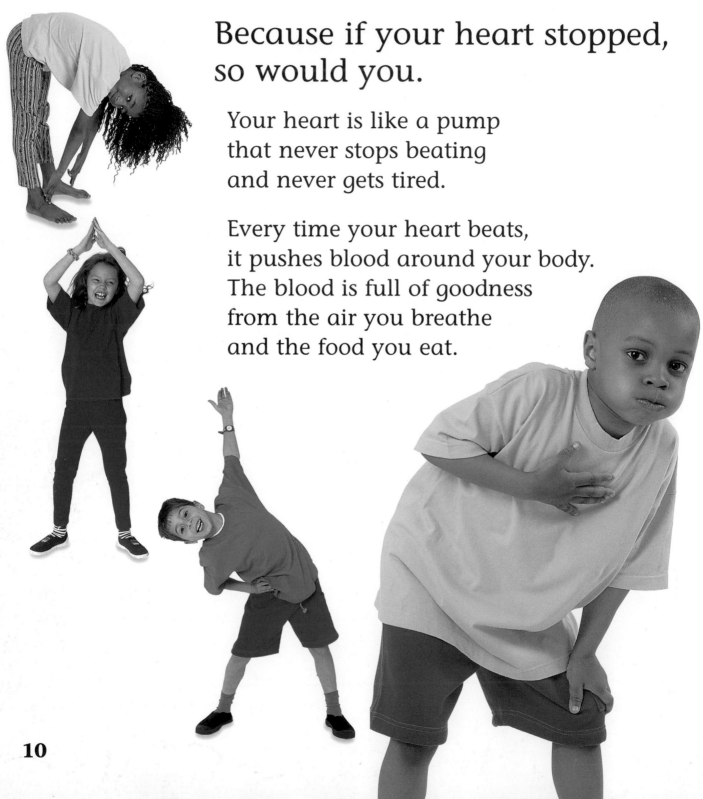

Why can't I hold my breath for very long?

Because you need to keep breathing to stay alive.

When you breathe in, you suck in air. Air has an invisible gas in it called oxygen, which your body needs.

When you breathe out, you push out stale air that your body no longer wants.

Why can't I see in the dark?

Because your eyes need light to see.

The black circles in your eyes
are holes called pupils.
Light comes into your eyes
through your pupils.

Why do I blink?

Because if you didn't,
your eyes would soon feel sore.

When you blink, your eyelids
are like windscreen wipers.
They wipe tears across your eyes.
This keeps them damp and free of dirt.

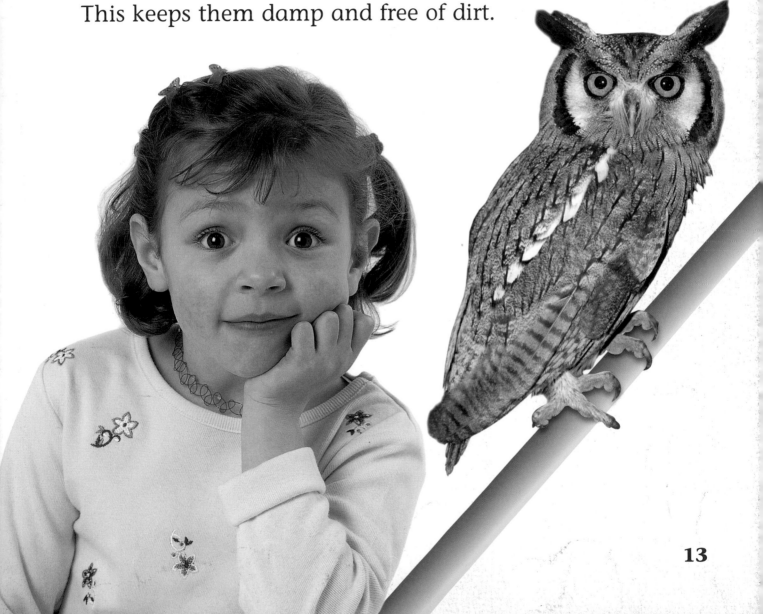

Why can't I eat just sweets?

Because you would
soon be ill.

Food is your body's fuel.
You need a mixture of different
foods to keep your body healthy.

Milk and meat help you grow.
Bread and pasta give you
lots of energy. Fruit and
vegetables keep you well.

Why can't I stop smelling things?

Because your nose is made for catching smells.

Millions of tiny hairs inside your nose catch smells. When you have a cold, your nose gets blocked up, so the hairs can't catch the smells around you.

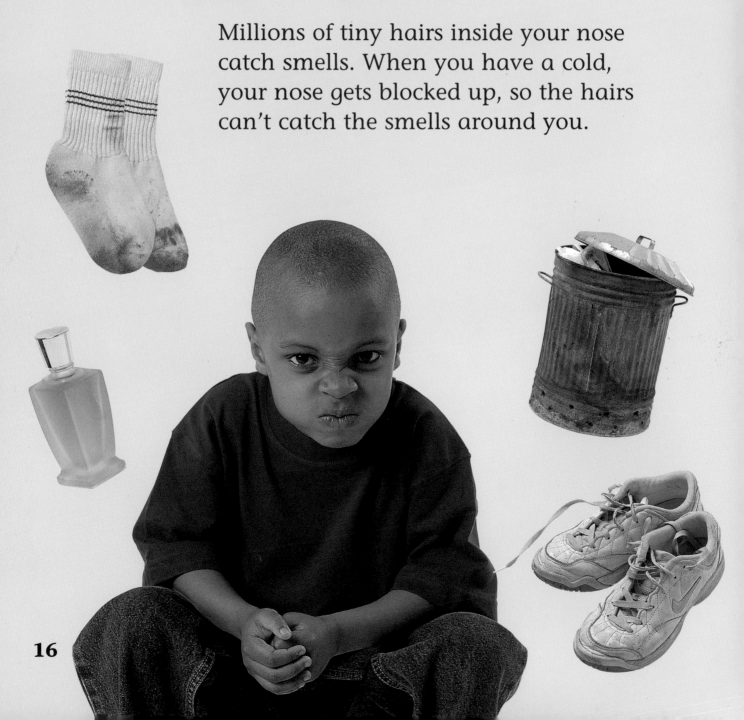

Why do I have to go to the loo?

Because your body needs to get rid of food and water it doesn't use.

Your body takes in goodness from your food and drink.

When you go to the loo, you get rid of any leftovers.

17

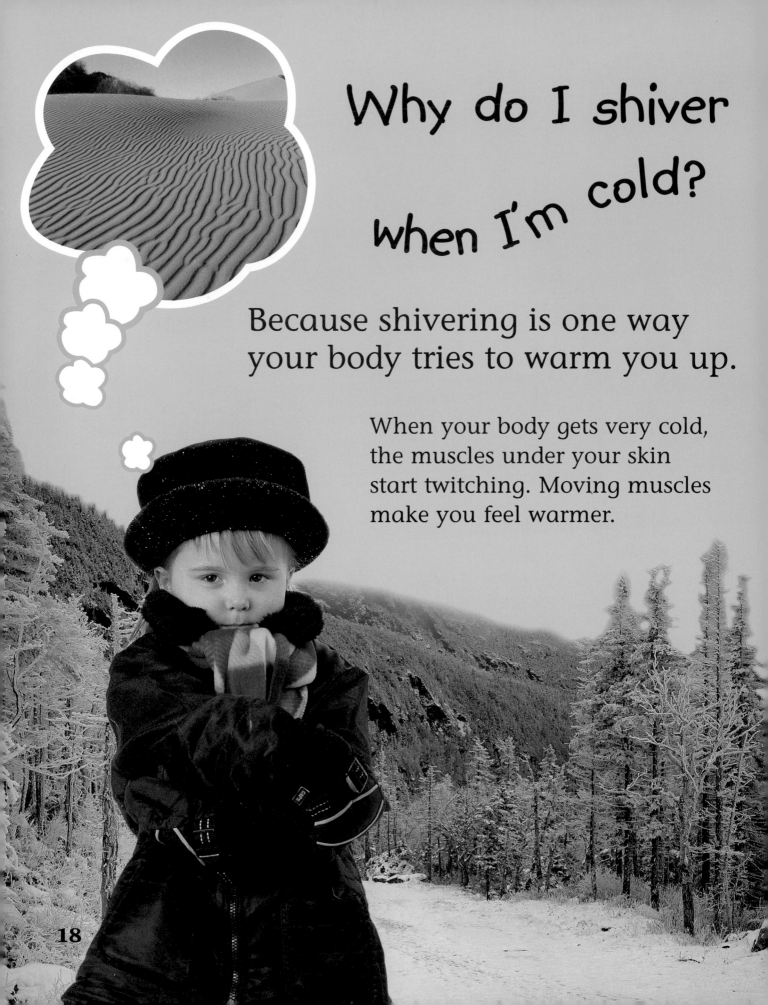

Why do I shiver when I'm cold?

Because shivering is one way your body tries to warm you up.

When your body gets very cold, the muscles under your skin start twitching. Moving muscles make you feel warmer.

18

Why do I sweat when I'm hot?

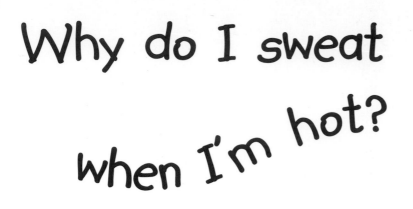

Because sweating is one way your body tries to cool you down.

Sweat is salty liquid. When you get very hot, it oozes out of tiny holes on to your skin.

When the sweat dries, it makes your body feel cooler.

Why do I have to wash?

Because if you didn't,
you would start to smell
very bad!

Dirt sticks to your skin.
The dirt contains
tiny living things,
which can make you
smelly or even ill.

When you have
a bath or shower
you wash them away.

Why can't I stay up all night?

Because your brain
and body need
a rest at the end
of the day.

While you are asleep,
your brain stops
thinking so hard and
your body slows down
and mends itself.

Why can't I stay young for ever?

Because you can't stop your body from changing.

Your body keeps growing and changing very slowly from the day you are born.

You will stop growing taller when you are about 18. But your body will never stop changing and you will never stop learning new things.

Body words

blood Blood carries important things such as oxygen and food to every part of your body.

bones The hard parts of your body. Your bones are joined together to make a framework called a skeleton.

brain The body's computer. It controls how your body works, and receives and sends messages to the rest of your body.

ear The body's microphone. It picks up sounds so that you can hear.

eye The body's camera. It lets in light so that you can see.

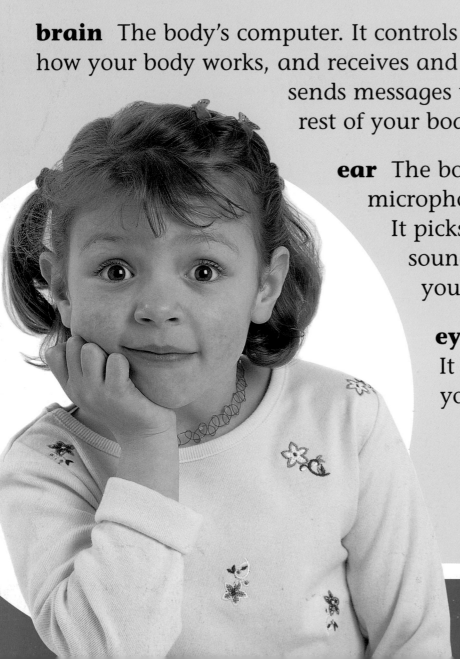

heart The body's pump. It sends blood all around your body.

joint The place where two bones meet. You can bend your body at the joints.

lungs The body's breathing machines. They supply your body with fresh oxygen and push out stale air.

muscles Things that move parts of your body.

All these words or phrases include a part of the body. Can you find out what they mean?

teeth

- by the skin of your teeth
- to have a sweet tooth

thumb

- thumbs up
- twiddle your thumbs

tongue

- to hold your tongue
- on the tip of the tongue
- tongue twister

eyes

- an eye opener
- eye-catching
- to keep your eyes peeled

nails

- nail-biting

ears

- within earshot
- prick up your ears
- in one ear and out at the other

breath
- out of breath
- save your breath
- hold your breath

hair
- let your hair down
- keep your hair on

heart
- learn by heart
- with all my heart

hand
- to lend a hand
- handmade

arm
- at arm's length
- with open arms

nose
- nosy
- to follow your nose

brain
- brainy
- brainwave

feet
- to put your foot down
- to find your feet

Notes for parents and teachers

Read this book through so that children become familiar with the ideas in it, and with specific words about the body. Then you may like to try out these activities that reinforce some of the ideas and give the children further talking points.

This is me
Talk to children about how they would describe themselves to someone who has never met them. Discuss their distinguishing details – the colour and length of their hair, the colour of their eyes, their favourite clothes. Ask them to make a colour picture or collage of themselves, which includes these details.

Eat up!
Look at the pictures of different foods in the book. Encourage children to think about other foods that help them grow, give them energy or keep them healthy. Ask children to draw a picture of their favourite meal on a paper plate or on a round piece of paper.

Wiggle waggle

Ask children to invent movements to exercise different parts of their body – including some unusual parts, such as the little toe, the chin or eyebrows, even the ears. They may enjoy doing this to music.

After their exercise, ask children what they notice about their bodies – are they hot, sweaty, breathing faster or tired? Can they think of any parts of the body that they didn't exercise? Can they think of any parts of the body they can't exercise (hair, nails, teeth)?

Growing all the time

Help children to compare photographs of themselves taken at different ages (especially baby photos and some taken most recently). Encourage them to talk about the differences they notice. How have their features, hair and bodies changed?

Talk about the things children are doing in the photos, so that they become aware of their changing abilities.

Index

Titles in the series

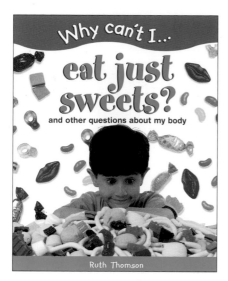

ISBN 1 84138 184 5 (hb)
ISBN 1 84138 377 5 (pb)
ISBN 1 84138 375 9 (big book)

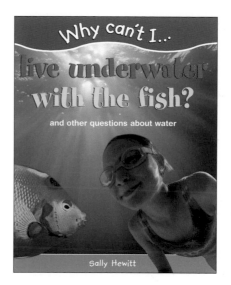

ISBN 1 84138 187 X (hb)
ISBN 1 84138 378 3 (pb)
ISBN 1 84138 376 7 (big book)

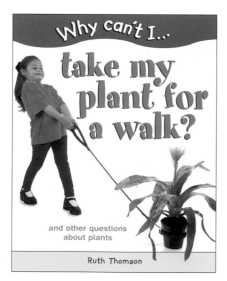

ISBN 1 84138 186 1 (hb)

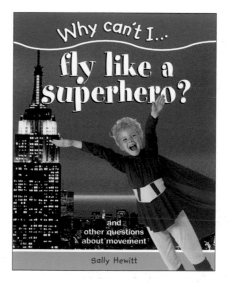

ISBN 1 84138 185 3 (hb)